PATHWAY ... S

He is Our Peace

EPHESIANS

BY DAVID JACKMAN

He is Our Peace
Pathway Bible Guides: Ephesians
© Matthias Media 2012

Matthias Media
(St Matthias Press Ltd ACN 067 558 365)
PO Box 225
Kingsford NSW 2032
Australia
Telephone: (02) 9663 1478; international: +61-2-9663-1478
Facsimile: (02) 9663 3265; international: +61-2-9663-3265
Email: info@matthiasmedia.com.au
Internet: www.matthiasmedia.com.au

Matthias Media (USA)
Telephone: 330 953 1702; international: +1-330-953-1702
Facsimile: 330 953 1712; international: +1-330-953-1712
Email: sales@matthiasmedia.com
Internet: www.matthiasmedia.com

ISBN 978 1 921896 40 8

Cover design and typesetting by Matthias Media.

CONTENTS

BEFORE YOU BEGIN

If asked to sum up in a word the experience of living in today's world, many millions of people might well choose the word 'brokenness'. In a fallen world, life frequently breaks down. Expectations are disappointed; tragedies strike; relationships break up; families disintegrate; hopes are smashed. Life is broken and it needs to be fixed—but how? All too often disappointment leads to bitterness, hurt to hostility, and cynicism morphs into aggression. We are all aware that 'Humpty' has 'had a great fall', but who can put the pieces of life back together again, and how might it happen?

Ephesians has God's answer. Many Christians affirm that this is a letter all about the church, and we shall certainly see why—but we are not its primary focus. It is supremely a letter about the Lord Jesus Christ, who is the head of his body, and from whom the whole church grows "so that it builds itself up in love" (4:16). This is a letter that teaches us about God's big purposes, on the grandest scale, here in time and stretching into eternity: "to unite all things in him [Christ]" (1:10). It exalts the Lord Jesus and shows us who he really is; what he has done for us, his people; and how the brokenness of our world can only be mended by the gospel of his grace.

If the greatest division of the first-century world—that between Jews and Gentiles—can be healed through the cross of Christ, then there are no broken relationships beyond his loving reach. Since Christ is our peace, reconciling sinful people like us to God as our Father, there can no longer be any barriers to separate us from one another once we are united to Jesus, by faith. The church of redeemed, reconciled believers then serves as a prototype, within time, of what God purposes to accomplish for all eternity. Loving relationships and unity between Christians are the fruit of the love of Christ for his people, seen in his death and resurrection. It is also the proof of his total supremacy over all the hostile powers of evil, including the devil himself, and the demonstration to the whole universe that God's mighty work of salvation is accomplished, that it is totally effective, and that it will be eternal in its outworking.

Studying this wonderful letter not only deepens our understanding of all that Jesus is and all that he has done for us, but also deepens our love for him. And that makes us want to live to please him, to walk in love as he loved us (5:2). As we study Paul's practical applications of the gospel to our new lifestyle, we shall be corrected, challenged and above all empowered to live an authentic Christian life in a broken world. Paul's purpose is that we should become more and more in practice what God has made us to be, and so reveal to the whole world the miracle of restoration and new life in Christ, which is the only cure for our human brokenness.

David Jackman
November 2011

1. CLEAR VISION

Ephesians 1:1-14

 Getting started

Christians often say that God is in control. But it's sometimes easier to say than believe. What is it that most makes you question whether God really is in control, either in the world at large, or in your personal life and circumstances?

Light from the Word

Read Ephesians 1:1-14.

1. The writer, readers and greeting are all related to Jesus Christ. What is the connection to Jesus in each case, and why do you think Paul draws attention to it (vv. 1-2)?

2. "In the heavenly places" is an unusual phrase (v. 3), indicating the nature of our spiritual blessings in Christ. What do you think it means? Check your answer out against its other uses in this letter (1:20, 2:6, 3:10, 6:12).

3. God chose his people before he made the world. What two great purposes does Paul highlight in verses 4-5? Why do they matter?

what did he create people for? .
Why did he create animals?

4. How does the fulfilment of these purposes add to the praise of God's grace (v. 6)?

5. Why are redemption and forgiveness so dependent on God's grace (v. 7)?

6. What do verses 8-9 teach us about how we came to know the "mystery" of God's will?

7. What is God's ultimate plan for his creation (v. 10)?

8. By "we" in verse 11, Paul seems to have himself and his fellow Jewish believers primarily in mind (contrast "you also" in verse 13, referring to the predominantly Gentile church). How does he describe God's blessings to them (vv. 11-12)?

9. What blessings do the Gentile believers now experience, and how have they come to receive them (vv. 13-14)?

 ## To finish

Look back on all the blessings listed in these verses, and remind yourself of how each one is dependent on Christ and being "in him". How does this help us with the issues raised in our 'Getting started' question? What sort of response do you think this passage calls for?

Give thanks and pray

- Thank God the Father for his wonderful cosmic plan of redemption, and the Lord Jesus for enabling it to happen through his sacrificial obedience to the cross.
- Pray for yourself and your church that you may understand the privilege of being caught up in God's eternal plan and that such clear vision will motivate all your choices and priorities.

•

2. CHRIST TRIUMPHANT

Ephesians 1:15-23

 **Getting started**

What things happen in our world that seem to indicate the forces of evil have the upper hand? Where does their power over us lie?

💡 Light from the Word

Read Ephesians 1:15-23.

1. Why is Paul so constantly thankful for his readers (vv. 15-16)?

2. What can we learn from Paul's prayer about *how* we can come to know God better (vv. 17-18a)?

3. What are the three aspects of God's grace in Christ that Paul wants his readers to know more fully (vv. 18b-19a)? What differences will they make in his readers' lives?

4. How are we helped to grasp more fully the greatness of God's power (vv. 19b-20)?

5. What difference does it make to life in this world that Jesus is exalted "in the heavenly places" (vv. 20-21)?

6. Putting verse 22 alongside verse 10, what do we learn about God's biggest picture, both now and in the 'not yet' of eternity?

7. Why is the present exaltation of the Lord Jesus "to [or for] the church" (v. 22)?

8. How is the church filled and completed by Christ (v. 23)? (See also 3:19 and 5:18.)

 ## To finish

Look back on all that these verses tell us about the Lord Jesus; what he has done and is doing for us, his people. Think particularly of how feeble the opposition really is in comparison to his mighty power. Refocus your answer to the 'Getting started' question in the light of what you have learned from this passage.

 ## Give thanks and pray

- Praise God for the exaltation and glory of the Lord Jesus as the result of his glorious triumph through his death and resurrection.
- Spend some time in worship and adoration of his majestic person and wonderful work.
- Pray Paul's prayer for the Spirit of wisdom and revelation, and for enlightened hearts, to know him better and to experience the hope and power that are vested in him alone.

3. RADICAL CHANGE

Ephesians 2:1-10

 **Getting started**

What strikes you most forcibly about the changes Christ has already made in your life? Are you still thanking him regularly for them?

💡 Light from the Word

Read Ephesians 2:1-10.

1. Verses 1-2 describe the deadness of the unbeliever in the midst of life. What are its symptoms and evidences?

2. Why could we never save ourselves (vv. 2-3)? How do we respond when people say the human race is getting better and better?

3. How do the world (v. 2), the flesh (v. 3) and the devil (v. 2) still influence human lives today? Are Christians immune?

4. What is the reason for the great change introduced in verse 4?

5. In verses 5-6, Paul outlines three aspects of God's rescuing work. What are they and how does each one affect our daily lives as Christians?

6. Re-read verses 4-7. From these verses, describe how the gospel brings glory to God.

7. What are the relative contributions of faith and works in our salvation and in living the Christian life (vv. 8-9)? What are the implications of this for our enjoyment and experience of God's grace in Christ?

8. How does verse 10 clinch the argument of this section, and what development does it add to our understanding?

 ## To finish

Think back over the great theological truths of these verses and try to relate them in practical ways to what you were before Christ met you, where you are now as a believer, and what your expectations of the future are. How does the study motivate you to be more thankful to God?

 ## Give thanks and pray

- Take time to thank God for his character revealed in the passage—his love, mercy, creative power, grace, kindness and foreknowledge.
- Pray that you will never forget the condition you were in when God raised you up.
- Ask God to show you the good works he has given you to do in your life now, and to give you his grace to do them.

4. ONE NEW MAN

Ephesians 2:11-22

 **Getting started**

What would make you break fellowship with any other real Christian, or prevent you from healing existing divisions?

☀ Light from the Word

Read Ephesians 2:11-22.

1. Although Paul has already stated that Jews and Gentiles in Christ are accepted by God on exactly the same grounds, here he reverts to the old Jewish vocabulary in referring to his Gentile friends (v. 11). What point is he making?

2. What does each of the pre-Christian disadvantages of the Gentiles imply about the state of the whole human race before God (v. 12)? How does each one, by contrast, highlight a blessing of the gospel?

3. What does it mean that Christ has become "our peace" and how did it happen (vv. 13-14a)?

4. How has Jesus abolished the law of commandments and ordinances by his death (v. 15)?

5. Why is it that only the cross unites believers from all sorts of ethnic backgrounds (v. 16)?

6. Verse 18 shows that each person of the Trinity is involved in our experience of peace and access (see also Romans 5:1-2). How does that work? And why do you think Paul stresses this to his Ephesian readers?

7. How can Christians be assured that we are all equally acceptable to God (vv. 19-20)?

8. What does the Old Testament imagery about the temple teach us about the church (vv. 21-22)? What do the present tenses imply?

 ## To finish

Though the division between Jewish and Gentile believers is not a major issue today in most places, yet there are still "dividing walls of hostility" which separate real Christians from one another—within churches or between churches. What are some of these that you encounter? How can the principles of this passage help us to challenge and seek to change these situations?

 ## Give thanks and pray

- Thank God for his great purpose that the church should demonstrate here, in time, the unity which will be fully accomplished when all things are shown to be united under Christ's feet in eternity.
- Ask God to help you, individually and as a group, to live out these realities more and more in specific situations where at present there is division.

5. MANIFOLD WISDOM

Ephesians 3

 ## Getting started

What do you think are the greatest personal needs you face in your life at the moment? How hopeful are you about them being met?

💡 Light from the Word

Read Ephesians 3:1-21.

1. What are the unique features of Paul's apostolic ministry (vv. 1-3), and why did the Ephesians need to be made aware of them?

2. How was the "mystery" revealed to Paul's readers (vv. 4-5)? (See also 2:20.)

3. What is the heart of the "mystery" (v. 6)?

4. How would verses 7-9 increase the reader's confidence in Paul and the message he preached?

5. What are the guarantees, in the present, of the certain future fulfilment of God's purposes (vv. 10-12)?

6. In verses 1-13, how does Paul encourage his readers not to look on his current imprisonment as a disaster? What might be the equivalent for us when we face adverse circumstances?

7. Try to express Paul's main request in verse 16 in your own words.

8. What does Paul hope for as the outcome of his prayer (vv. 17-19)?

9. How does our deepening knowledge of God's love (v. 19) lead us to maturity?

10. What are the encouragements to keep praying contained in the doxology of verses 20-21?

 ## To finish

The first half of this chapter is very 'big picture', dealing with God's eternal plan to reveal the "mystery of Christ" and its outworking in the lives of the Ephesian readers. As Paul moves on to pray for them in the second half of the chapter, these huge and eternal dimensions of the gospel form the basis of his prayer.

How do you think the passage would have helped Paul's readers face the hostile pagan culture of Ephesus? How does it help you to face the needs and anxieties you raised at the beginning of this study?

 ## Give thanks and pray

- Praise God for all the blessings of the gospel and Christian living that are listed in this chapter, which come to us purely as a result of God's grace.
- Pray for one another that on the basis of this confidence, the requests of verses 16-19 will become increasingly realized in your fellowship together and in your ongoing witness and service.
- Read verses 20-21 together as a joint expression of your faith and as a closing benediction.

6. ACTIVE UNITY

Ephesians 4:1-16

 **Getting started**

What do you value most about your fellowship with other believers, in the life of your local church? Where might there be room for improvement?

💡 Light from the Word

Read Ephesians 4:1-16.

1. In verse 1, Paul urges his readers to "walk in a manner worthy" of the calling they have received (some translations have "live a life worthy"). This verb ('to walk') is used quite a few times in the letter. Look up 2:1-3, 10; especially 4:17; and 5:2, 8, 15 to understand more fully what a life "worthy of the calling to which you have been called" means (v. 1).

2. Why do you think the qualities listed in verses 2-3 are marks of a godly life, and what is surprising about the list?

3. List all the reasons or factors that generate unity (vv. 4-6). Why do you think Paul is so concerned about this issue?

4. What does the variety of God's grace-gifts in verses 7-11 tell us about diversity and unity in the church?

5. Based on verse 12, are the word ministry gifts an end in themselves? And what does this imply for our practice and evaluation of their use?

6. What are the indicators of spiritual maturity for which God looks in a local congregation? In what ways do these characteristics cast a good light on the gospel for a watching world?

7. In verse 15, Paul turns "truth" into a verb ("truthing in love") so that it seems to involve more than just speaking. What might this active "truthing" look like and what will it achieve?

8. Identify the ingredients of a healthy, functioning congregation (v. 16). How can you help your local fellowship to grow more into this fulfilment, using what you have gained from this study?

 # To finish

Using the last part of question 6, reflect on ways in which local churches can either forward or hinder the cause of the gospel according to their relational unity or divisions. Why should the watching world think that we are anything more than a religious club of reasonably like-minded people if our churches do not demonstrate the magnetic love and grace which, we claim, are the essence of the gospel we preach? How does the teaching of Ephesians 1-3 help to lift our understanding to the eternal perspective of the church in God's purposes (e.g. 1:22-23, 3:10)? And how does that motivate us to work much harder (see 4:3) at a loving, active and truth-based unity in the gospel among all true believers? Discuss practical ideas as to how this can be developed both in your group and in your wider church fellowship.

 # Give thanks and pray

- Give thanks for all the "truthing in love" that you can already see in your own fellowship.
- Thank God again for his great purpose in calling together an international and numberless community of believers, and for the privilege of being part of such a big picture, which is eternal.
- Ask God to show you areas where you need to work hard both to maintain the unity he has already given, and also to reach the unity he holds before us, in terms of our personal and joint maturity in Christ.
- Ask for his strength to act upon this in the coming days.

7. RENEWED MINDS

Ephesians 4:17-5:2

 Getting started

Why do we find it so difficult to make the connection between the truth we know and the daily lives we lead?

💡 Light from the Word

Read Ephesians 4:17-5:2.

1. In 4:17 and following, why do you think Paul turns back for a third time to the way his Gentile readers used to live? Compare 2:1-3 and 2:11-12.

2. Ephesians 4:17-19 forms a tightly argued paragraph. Look at it closely and see if you can trace the connections between mind, heart and behaviour.

3. How might this understanding of how human beings 'work' help us in our evangelism?

4. What does 4:20-21 tell us about how we come to know Christ? How have you seen this working out in your experience?

5. Identify the three ingredients of change, from Gentile living to Christian transformation, in 4:22-24. What is the key, central requirement (4:23), and why is it so important?

6. Ephesians 4:25-32 works through the three principles of 4:22-24 with five specific areas of behaviour. Fill in the following table.

	What needs to be "put away"?	What should replace it?	New mindset that motivates/ enables
4:25			
4:26-27			
4:28			
4:29-30			
4:31-32			

7. How does this section help us to understand better how to connect our belief and our behaviour?

8. What do we learn in 5:1-2 about how 'walking' (or living) in love can increasingly be our own experience?

 ## To finish

Look back at what this passage has taught us about how the mind (our thinking) affects our life experience (behaviour)—before we turned to Christ (4:17-19) and now (4:20ff). List the encouragements in these verses that motivate us to put off the old self and put on the new.

Give thanks and pray

- Be thankful for the specific detail of these verses in explaining to us what "true righteousness and holiness" look like in everyday terms.
- Pray through the key areas of your behaviour, in terms of your speech, emotional reactions, attitude to possessions and personal relationships. Where do you need to repent? What areas do you need to ask God to renew? What actions do you need his power to take, so that you move from the truth you know to the life you lead?
- Pray the prayer of 3:17b-19, that you may live a life of love.

8. GODLY LIVING
Ephesians 5:3-21

 **Getting started**

Looking back over recent weeks or months, can you identify any areas where you think you have made progress in fighting against the world, the flesh and the devil? What factors have helped you most to advance in godliness?

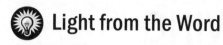 **Light from the Word**

Read Ephesians 5:3-21.

1. Putting verses 3 and 5 together and remembering what Paul has just been teaching in 5:1-2, why must the sins in these verses be eradicated from the Christian community?

2. How does Paul suggest we can protect ourselves from drifting back to our pre-Christian lifestyle (v. 4)?

3. In verses 5-6, how does Paul help us to recognize ways we might deceive ourselves, or be deceived by others, into thinking that these sins are not such a big deal?

4. In verses 7-8, Paul emphasizes the total contrast between darkness and light. Notice that does he not say "you are in the light", but "you *are* light". What does that mean? (See also Matthew 5:13-16.)

5. Verses 11-14 describe the process by which the works of darkness are to be avoided and exposed. What are the ingredients of this, and what do they imply for our lives in our society today?

6. What are the marks of walking wisely (vv. 15-17)? How can we encourage one another to live this way?

7. In the light of 1:23 and 3:19, what do you think Paul's exhortation to be filled with (or 'by') the Spirit means (v. 18)? Why does he contrast it with being drunk?

8. What are the continuing evidences of the ongoing filling by the Spirit in us, as individuals and as a church (vv. 19-21)? If you were compiling a list of what it meant to be 'Spirit-filled', is this you would have written? Why/why not?

To finish

In this passage, who is responsible for us coming to know the truth and then living out that truth in our lives?

How does the passage help us to get on to the front foot, and not merely be reactive and defensive in our encounter with the powers of evil? Do you need to make some changes of attitude in your own walk and warfare?

Give thanks and pray

- Take time to rejoice in God, who is light and in whom is no darkness at all, and to praise him for the revelation of his glory in the person of our Lord Jesus Christ.
- Ask him to keep you from double-mindedness and compromise, to save you from being deceived by the plausible rebellion of the culture in which we live.
- Pray for wisdom and understanding to know what is best, in all your changing and challenging circumstances, and then for dependence on his Holy Spirit to empower you with the very life of God, so that you may live in the fullness of his love. And take time to be thankful (see verses 4 and 20)!

9. FAMILY CIRCLES

Ephesians 5:22-6:9

 Getting started

Relationships in marriage and family life in our society are generally a long way from the principles laid down here. What are prevailing dominant views in our culture about how husbands and wives, and parents and children, should relate?

💡 Light from the Word

Read Ephesians 5:22-6:9.

1. Is 5:22-24 teaching that a Christian wife must do everything her husband may demand? How does the connection back to 5:21 and 5:18 help us to understand these verses?

2. Look again at 5:22-24 and work out how the church's relationship with Christ helps us to understand what this sort of godly submission actually involves.

3. Similarly, how does the parallel between Christ and the church help us to understand what a Christian husband's love for his wife should be like (5:25-27)?

4. What added motivations does 5:28-30 provide for the distinctive love of a Christian husband for his wife?

5. What would be the implications of the quotation from Genesis 2:24 (5:31) for these Gentile Christians in Ephesus? Is marriage to be modelled on the gospel, or is the gospel an illustration of marriage?

6. From 6:1-3, what characteristics of discipleship should Christian children demonstrate in their life at home?

7. How might a Christian father fail or provoke his children (6:4)? What is the remedy?

8. List the motivations for the Christian to live obediently at work (6:5-8). How does this translate to today?

9. How might the Christian employer fail his workers? What will enable him to avoid that sort of behaviour (6:9)?

🕮 To finish

At the heart of Ephesus and its culture stood the statue and temple of the great goddess Diana (Artemis), the 'queen of the cosmos', the 'saviour of the universe', the goddess of fertility. It is not surprising that the most detailed New Testament instruction on Christian marriage is given in this context, since what Paul is advocating directly undermines these pagan values and practices, on which the wealth of Ephesus depended. As in the 21st-century Western world, so in the first-century world—to become a Christian was to espouse a totally different set of sexual ethics. How could we demonstrate in our marriages and families the better way of the Creator's instructions, to challenge and illuminate the chaos of our contemporary situation? What rationale would we give to those who question why we take a passage like this so seriously? What will we teach our children to answer when they face these issues?

Give thanks and pray

- Praise God, not only that he loves but also that he *is* love. Thank him for the dynamic of personal interactive love that is at the heart of the Trinity, in whose life we are called to be partakers.
- Pray for that love to animate the marriage relationships and family circles represented by your group.
- Ask God to fill you with his Spirit so that the patterns outlined here may be translated into reality increasingly in your life, and so shine the light of God's purposes for all human relationships into the darkness of our cultural relativism.

10. SPIRITUAL WARFARE

Ephesians 6:10-24

 Getting started

Do you view your daily life as a cosmic spiritual conflict? What is your reaction to this perspective—exaggerated, scary, dispiriting?

☀ Light from the Word

Read Ephesians 6:10-24.

1. In verse 10, Paul reminds us of the major theme of the Lord's power, which has threaded through the whole letter. Remind yourself of some of the previous teaching by re-visiting 1:18-21; 3:16, 20-21; and 5:18. Jot down some of the main points.

2. What do verses 11-12 teach us about the battle we are in? What are our tactics to be?

3. Why does Paul say that the aim of our warfare is to stand (v. 13)? Why not to advance?

4. Paul uses the image of a well-armed Roman soldier to teach us of all the resources God provides for the battle (vv. 14-17). By using the references below to these major elements of our Christian weaponry, build up your picture of what is involved in putting on this gospel armour, making notes as you go.

- Truth (1:13; 4:15, 21, 24-25; 5:9)

- Righteousness (4:24, 5:9)

- Peace (2:14-18, 4:3)

- Faith (1:1, 13, 15, 19; 2:8; 3:12, 17; 4:5, 13)

- Salvation (1:13; 2:5, 8; 5:23)

- The word of God (1:13, 5:26)

5. In verses 14-17, what are we to defend against and how are we to attack?

6. Note the repetition of "all" in verse 18. What are the practical implications of Paul's stress on the totality of prayer in the spiritual warfare?

7. What does Paul pray for himself (vv. 19-20)? What lessons about gospel work can we learn from this emphasis?

8. What impression do you have from verses 21-23 about the relationship the apostle has with his readers? What can we learn from it?

9. What is the emphasis within verse 24 and why does the letter end on this note?

 To finish

Returning to the 'Getting started' question, how have your original reactions been challenged, changed, reinforced or deepened as a result of studying this final section of Ephesians? What practical differences will this make in your daily life?

Thinking back over the 'big picture' of Ephesians, what has stuck in your mind? If you had to choose a key verse to sum up the message of Ephesians, what would it be?

Give thanks and pray

- Take time to thank God for his amazing plan of salvation in the Lord Jesus.
- Praise him that all the hostile powers have been conquered through his cross and resurrection and that nothing can overcome God's power, harm his people, or frustrate his purposes.
- Praise him for the resources of the whole armour of God and for the power of the Holy Spirit, accessed through the Word and prayer.
- Ask God that, in the light of all you have learned, you may increasingly "walk in a manner worthy of the calling to which you have been called" (4:1).

Feedback on this resource

We really appreciate getting feedback about our resources—not just suggestions for how to improve them, but also positive feedback and ways they can be used. We especially love to hear that the resources may have helped someone in their Christian growth.

You can send feedback to us via the 'Feedback' menu in our online store, or write to us at PO Box 225, Kingsford NSW 2032, Australia.

FOR THE LEADER

What are Pathway Bible Guides?

The Pathway Bible Guides aim to provide simple, straightforward Bible study material for:

- Christians who are new to studying the Bible (perhaps because they've been recently converted or because they have joined a Bible study group for the first time)
- Christians who find other studies[1] too much of a stretch.

Accordingly, we've designed the studies to be short, straightforward and easy to use, with a simple vocabulary. At the same time, we've tried to do justice to the passages being studied, and to model good Bible-reading principles. We've tried to be simple without being simplistic; no-nonsense without being no-content.

The questions and answers assume a small group context, but it should be easy to adapt them to suit different situations, such as individual study and one-to-one.

Your role as leader

Because many in your group may not be used to reading and discussing a Bible passage in a group context, a greater level of responsibility will fall to you as the leader of the discussions. There are the usual responsibilities of preparation, prayer and managing group dynamics. In addition, there will be an extra dimension of forming and encouraging good Bible reading habits in people who may not have much of an idea of what those habits look like.

Questions have been kept deliberately brief and simple. For this reason, you may have to fill in some of the gaps that may have been addressed in, say, an Interactive Bible Study. Such 'filling in' may take the form of asking follow-up questions, or using your best judgement to work out when you might need to supply background information. That sort of information, and some suggestions about other questions you could ask, may be found in the following leader's notes. In addition, a *New Bible Dictionary* is always a useful aid to preparation, and simple commentaries such as those in the *Tyndale* or *Bible Speaks Today* series are often helpful. On Ephesians, the commentaries by Peter O'Brien, Leon Morris and John Stott are all good.[2] Consult these resources after you have done your own preparation.

On the question of background information, these studies are written from the assumption that God's word stands alone. God works through his Holy Spirit and the leaders he has gifted—such as you—to make his meaning clear. Assuming this to be true, the best interpreter and provider of background information for Scripture will not be academic historical research, but Scripture itself. Extra historical information may be useful for the purpose of illustration, but it is unnecessary for understanding and applying what God says to us.

The format of the studies

The discussion questions on each passage follow a simple pattern. There is a question at the beginning of each discussion that is intended to get people talking around the issues raised by the passage, and to give you some idea of how people are thinking. If the group turns out to be confident, motivated and comfortable with each other and the task at hand, you may even decide to skip this question.

Alternatively, if the group members are shy or quiet, you may decide to think of related types of questions that you could add in to the study, so as to maintain momentum in a non-threatening way.

After the first question, the remaining questions work through the passage sequentially, alternating between observation, interpretation and application in a way that will become obvious when you do your own preparation. The final question of each discussion, just before the opportunity for prayer, could be used in some groups to encourage (say) one person each week to give a short talk (it could be 1 minute or 5 minutes, depending on the topic and the people). The thinking here is that there's no better way to encourage understanding of a passage than to get people to the point where they can explain it to others. Use your judgement in making the best use of this final exercise each week, depending on the people in your group.

In an average group, it should be possible to work through the study in approximately 45 minutes. But it's important that you work out what your group is capable of, given the time available, and make adjustments accordingly. Work out in advance which questions or sub-points can be omitted if time is short.

And have a few supplementary questions or discussion starters up your sleeve if your group is dealing with the material quickly and hungering for more. Each group is different. It's your job as leader to use the printed material as 'Bible Guides', and not as a set of questions that you must rigidly stick to regardless of your circumstances.

Preparation: 60/40/20

Ideally, group members should spend half an hour reading over the passage and pencilling in some answers *before* they come to the group. Not every group member will do this, of course, but encourage them with the idea that the more they prepare for the study, the more they will get out of the discussion.

In terms of your own preparation as leader, we recommend you put aside approximately *two hours*, either all at once or in two one-hour blocks, and that you divide up the time as follows:

- 60 minutes reading the passage and answering the questions yourself as best you can (without looking at the leader's notes or Bible commentaries)
- 40 minutes consulting the leader's notes (plus other resources, like commentaries). Add to your own answers, and jot down supplementary questions or other information that you want to have available as you lead the discussion. Make sure you write everything you need on the study pages—the last thing you want to do is to keep turning to the 'answers' in the back during the group discussion
- 20 minutes praying about the study and for your group members.

This 60/40/20 pattern will help you to focus on the Bible and what it's saying, rather than simply regurgitating to the group what is in the leader's notes. Remember, these notes are just that—notes to offer some help and guidance. They are not the Bible! As a pattern of preparation, 60/40/20 also helps you to keep praying for yourself and your group, that God would give spiritual growth as his word is sown in your hearts (see Luke 8:4-15; 1 Cor 3:5-7).

If, for some reason, you have less or more time to spend in preparation, simply apply the 60/40/20 proportions accordingly.

1. Such as the Interactive Bible Study (IBS) series also available from Matthias Media.
2. L Morris, *Expository Reflections on the Letter to the Ephesians*, Baker, Grand Rapids, 1994; P O'Brien, *The Letter to the Ephesians*, PNTC, Apollos, Leicester, 1999; J Stott, *The Message of Ephesians*, BST, IVP, Leicester, 1979.

1. CLEAR VISION

Ephesians 1:1-14

▶ Remember 60/40/20

 Getting started

It is so easy to take our world view from the pressures of our culture, whether through the media or personal contacts. The 'Getting started' question is designed to get us looking inside first to see where our doubts and fears are about God being in charge, and then to prepare us for the panoramic views of spiritual reality that the study passages open up for us.

Studying the passage

The greeting that begins any New Testament letter is always more than just a standard 'hello'. The identity of the author and the letter's destination are basic, but what are the distinctives that the writer emphasizes? Here it is not so much the greeting itself (v. 2), which is comparatively conventional (though note that the full title of "the Lord Jesus Christ" is used), but rather it is Paul's emphasis on his divinely-given authority as an apostle (v. 1a), and his reminder that Christians live at two addresses—they are "in Ephesus", and they are "in Christ Jesus". The interaction between the two leads us into the letter's major concerns.

Verse 3 introduces an unusual phrase, "in the heavenly places", which is so important to the letter that it is worthwhile even at this early stage stopping off to look at its other uses in Ephesians (question 2). Encourage the group to think it means not just "heaven" (see 6:12), but also the whole unseen domain of spiritual forces, where a cosmic conflict is being fought out in which we too are involved. It's probably unwise to allow too much speculation at this point, but the issue needs to be noted since so much of the rest of the letter deals with it.

Verses 3-14 form one long sentence in the original, so the ideas do need to be kept closely together. We need to remember that it is actually one long benediction, in which Paul blesses God for all the spiritual benefits he has given so lavishly to his people. Questions 3-9 are designed to pull out the detail from the verses of what Paul means by "in Christ with every spiritual blessing" (v. 3).

It would be easy for the group to become stuck in speculative discussion about election and predestination (v. 4), but Paul's concern is the reality and purpose of these great truths, not abstract theologizing. You will need to keep the group on track here. Probably the best way of doing this is to draw attention to the "in Christ" theme, which dominates the paragraph. Christ is referred to either by name or reference in every single verse up to verse 13, with the exception of verse 8. This is a magnificent section establishing and elevating the Lord Jesus Christ in all his majestic splendour and rescuing grace, so we want to come out of the study thrilled with who we are in him and with our eyes fixed on Jesus and our faith deepened so that we have total confidence in his person and work.

Another way to avoid getting bogged down in the intricacies of predestination is to underline with the group the purposes of God in bestowing all these spiritual blessings on his people. Some are for our direct benefit in terms of holy living, divine sonship (vv. 4-5), forgiveness (v. 7), wisdom and insight (v. 8), and in the revelation of God's mind and purposes (v. 9). But running all the way through (vv. 6, 12, 14) is the greater purpose of "the praise of his glory", revealed in his grace. Paul wants his readers to be assured in their understanding and reception of all the gospel benefits they have received by God's sovereign grace "in Christ", because he knows that is how they will live distinctively different lives to God's glory, in Ephesus or anywhere else. It is central to the purpose of the passage to keep these practical perspectives clearly in view as we rejoice in the detail of all that Christ has accomplished for his people. As the passage moves from God's sovereign choice in time past to the experience of the Christian believer in the present, note that everything depends on the cross (v. 7). It is easy to pass over the phrase "through his blood" but it is the key to understanding God's grace (question 5).

This section is one of the 'mountain peaks' of New Testament pastoral theology, so don't be surprised if it is hard to do it justice in one study. Its content is far bigger than we can grasp. But if you plan to cover each part equally and keep the study moving on so as not to be sidetracked from the big picture, you will have served the group well. It is particularly important to be aware of the movement of the passage towards the climax in verse 10b. As you read from verse 9, you have a sense of Paul building up to this great revelation (and it is truly staggering in its applications). One way in which this happens is by the introduction of the word "mystery" in verse 9, which will occur again at 3:3, 4, 9; 5:32 and 6:19. Since Bible words have Bible meanings it is always more valuable to understand a term's significance by observing its usage in the letter, rather than simply looking up its derivation in a lexicon. Such a "mystery" could only be understood by revelation, which is the disclosure of God's biggest purpose for planet earth, both for time and eternity, the 'now' and the 'not yet' (v. 10a). This purpose is nothing less than "to unite all things in him, things in heaven and things on earth [i.e. everywhere]" (v. 10b). Do take time at question 7 to meditate on the implications of this both for our world view and for our personal priorities in life.

Study 2 will show us that Christ is already appointed to be head over everything for the church (1:22), so this is clearly the present reality as 1:20-21 will make plain. But here in 1:10 the stress is more on the future fulfilment of this great plan, when Christ's victory will be exercised over the whole of creation, when every knee will bow and every tongue confess the lordship of Jesus (Phil 2:9-11). Ephesus was full of "mystery" religions and cults, each with their own views of the meaning of existence and the purpose of the universe, but Paul wants his readers to be certain that those questions and searchings all find their fulfilment in Christ and in the gospel.

The final verses therefore come right down to the present experience of the writer and his readers in first-century Ephesus (vv. 11-14). As question 8 indicates, the "we" of verse 11 seems to refer to the priority of the Jews, in chronological terms, in receiving God's revelation in Jesus. The "you also" in verse 13 is most naturally read as referring to the Gentiles' inclusion "in Christ" through Paul's own missionary apostleship (see Acts 19). The Lord Jesus came first to "the lost sheep of the house of Israel" (Matt 10:6), which is where faith and hope "in Christ" first was generated. But Paul's overriding purpose is to assure the predominantly Gentile Ephesian believers that their privileges are exactly the same, and that they are in no way inferior to Jewish believers, or less secure.

Note in verses 13-14 a summary of what it means to be "in Christ": the gospel word of truth is heard and believed; then the Holy Spirit is received, as a present mark of God's possession and a deposit guaranteeing future glory, in the fullness of redemption. The implications work out in two ways: we are now

God's possession, or inheritance; and all that he has for his redeemed people will certainly one day be ours.

 ## To finish

So many Christians fail to realize and so appropriate all the gospel blessings that are already ours "in Christ". It would be like receiving a large legacy cheque and being grateful for it, treasuring it even, but framing it and putting it on the wall rather than cashing it and living in the enjoyment of all its benefits. The 'cash value' of this passage is immense in terms of faith, joy and peace, not only in our personal lives as we seek to live for Christ in our 'Ephesus', but also in the church for our corporate faith and enthusiastic witness.

 ## Give thanks and pray

Each study will end with a suggestion for thanksgiving and for prayer. These are intended only as a starting point. However, it is good to model thanksgiving and prayer that flow from what is learnt in the Bible study.

2. CHRIST TRIUMPHANT

Ephesians 1:15-23

▶ Remember 60/40/20

 Getting started

We know from Acts 19:18-19 that Ephesus was a hotbed of occult practices and that many of the first converts to Christ were from this background. They would need to know that none of the hostile powers had any authority over them, since they were "in Christ" and he is at God's right hand "far above all" (Eph 1:20-21). The total victory of Jesus gives his people security and confidence to live godly lives in a rebellious world, whatever the opposition, which is a lesson as much needed in the 21st century as in the first century. Our view of Christ's majesty and power is often very limited by time and visibility, and we need the mind-expanding truths of this magnificent section.

Studying the passage

This remaining section of chapter 1 is again one long sentence in the original. It is also presented in the form of a prayer (v. 16), though verses 15-17 are more in the form of a personal report. Either way, we learn the concerns Paul had for the Ephesian believers, which clearly became the focus for his intercessions on their behalf. Not only does he tell them what he is praying for them, but the content of his prayer is also clearly a major teaching ingredient of the letter. So these verses have a double agenda. Firstly, we learn what it means to know Christ better (v. 17), which is to appreciate who Jesus is, where he is now and what are the benefits of his grace in the present. But also we see the sort of prayers we should be praying for one another so that mind and heart, understanding and experience, are united in a life of assured faith and hope, sharing in "the immeasurable greatness of his power" (v. 19).

Verse 15 reminds us that faith in Christ and love for Christians are the Pauline marks of genuine new birth, whether in Jews or Gentiles. The verse indicates that many of Paul's readers were unknown to him, although Acts 19:10 tells us that he spent at least two years in Ephesus. This probably indicates that the letter had a much wider circulation in the hinterland of the city and other more outlying house churches in Asia Minor. It is no reason to question the Pauline authorship or the primary Ephesian destination, even though some manuscripts do not include "Ephesus" in 1:1. Paul's thankfulness for genuine gospel growth is always balanced by earnest prayer for the continued health and development of the young Christians and their churches (v. 16).

Verses 17-23 are probably best divided into two sections with regard to their thought-flow. The division occurs in verse 19, where Paul's prayer for his readers to know God's power in the first half of the verse triggers a more detailed exposition of what that power is and how it is currently evidenced (vv. 19b-23).

The first half of the paragraph (vv. 17-19a) has two major requests, each governed by a "so that" clause, indicating purpose or result. It will be important for the group to identify the structure in order to appreciate the logic of the teaching, so without getting too enmeshed in structure, take a minute or two to point out how the sentence 'works'. In verse 17, Paul is asking for "the Spirit [or a spirit] of wisdom and of revelation" and in verse 18a for enlightened hearts. Both of these are gifts of God, as are the spiritual blessings of 1:3-14. Paul recognizes that the Holy Spirit is the only source of understanding and enlightenment through the divine revelation, and that is what he is asking for (question 2). Note also that there is no divorce here between the work of the Spirit and wisdom/knowledge; nor should we drive a wedge between the Spirit and the Word—as if the Spirit gives us different knowledge than we get from the Word. The word of God is the sword of the Spirit that he wields in our hearts and lives (see 6:17).

In question 3, the outcome Paul desires is a deeper, relational knowledge of God (v. 17b), and a fuller heart understanding (in the control centre of the personality) of what the future holds for God's people and the incomparable power which can bring it all to fruition (vv. 18b-19a). Note that the phrase "glorious inheritance in the saints" may well mean that Christians are God's inheritance, through Christ's redemptive work. We are more accustomed to thinking of our inheritance "that is imperishable, undefiled, and unfading, kept in heaven for you" (1 Pet 1:4), and this is gloriously true. But here the thought may be nearer to Exodus 19:5 where Israel, redeemed from Egypt by the blood of the Passover lambs, is referred to as the Lord's "treasured possession", his personal treasure chest, or as we might say his 'investment portfolio'.

From verse 19b the focus is on the nature and scope of the divine power (question 4). The verse contains most of the power vocabulary of the New Testament. Four words are used to describe its superlative dimensions, counteracting perhaps the four categories of potential opposition detailed in verse 21. Certainly, the overall effect is one of irresistible might. But we must not miss the point that what guarantees this amazing claim to total authority and power is not a theological argument, but a fact of history—the resurrection of Christ (v. 20). Just as in study 1 we saw that the cross was the central ingredient of God's redemptive strategy (1:7), so now the other side of that great rescue event—the empty tomb and the risen Lord—is the guarantee of our present security and wonderful eternal future.

The implications of this total victory are the focus of verses 21-23 and of questions 5-8. The four descriptions of the hostile powers (human and spiritual) in verse 21 are designed to be all-inclusive. Jesus has conquered death and the devil and so is "far above" them all, whatever their pretensions (see also 1:10; 2:2; 3:10, 15; 4:8, 27; 6:11-12, 16). Paul's readers have nothing to fear from the occult powers that so dominated life in Ephesus and to which they were once enslaved.

The victory of Jesus in verse 22 is "to the church" or "for the church" (NIV), now as well as eternally. Because Jesus reigns now and his people are united to him, as the body to its head, all the divine grace of God in Christ is able to be communicated to believers. The concept of verse 23 becomes the prayer of 3:19.

This begins to develop the increasingly important theme in the letter that it is in the church that God's true grace and power can be seen to be at work (see 2:14-17, 19; 3:10). The church is the present focus of what will be revealed in the whole creation, at the end. Everything is under Christ's feet, brought together under his lordship (1:9-10).

 ## To finish

Much of the value of this study is to refocus our minds on the greatness of Christ, his majestic rule and limitless power, so that we begin to review the problems of living in our 'Ephesus' in this revolutionary perspective. We only fear men when we forget God. We show that we have not forgotten God when prayer of this sort for one another characterizes our group and church fellowship.

3. RADICAL CHANGE

Ephesians 2:1-10

▶ Remember 60/40/20

 ## Getting started

The Ephesian believers really need to know how radical and deep is the change that they have experienced. It is literally a new life that they are now living. "You were dead" (v. 1) is contrasted with "But God... made us alive together with Christ" (vv. 4-5). Paul's description of their earlier state (vv. 1-3) is particularly Ephesian in its expression, as we recall that their city was dominated by the massive statue and temple of Diana (Artemis) and her occult religion. It is only when we are aware of how much God has done for us in Christ that we are likely to be committed to living godly lives, for as Jesus said, "he who is forgiven little, loves little" (Luke 7:47).

Studying the passage

Verses 1-7 form one long sentence in the original, in the course of which we move from death in sin (v. 1) to life "in the heavenly places" in Christ Jesus (v. 6).

We have already had the contrast between "we" in 1:11, referring to Paul and the original Jewish believers, and "you" in 1:13, meaning the Gentile converts. This is now developed in 2:1-2 ("And you"), although Paul does not exclude himself in verse 3 ("we all"). These verses (1-3) are true of us all, but perhaps verse 2 has a special Gentile/Ephesian focus, with its emphasis on their bondage to the spiritual forces of evil under "the prince of the power of the air" (i.e. the devil).

The word 'walk' in verse 2 (or 'live' in the NIV) occurs elsewhere in the letter at 2:10; 4:1, 17; 5:2, 8, 15. Its idea of continuous movement makes it suitable as a synonym for habitual lifestyle.

Note the unholy trio of the world, the flesh and the devil, who are the occupying forces, aiming to keep the unbeliever in a state of spiritual deadness through sin (question 2). It will be helpful to discuss how these external pressures combine with internal rebellion to have the same effect on unbelievers today (question 3).

"But God…" (v. 4) presents one of the most glorious contrasts in the whole of the New Testament. Note the emphasis on God's initiative in the great rescue mission, which is the expression of his character of love and mercy. There is also a characteristic Ephesian mention of the dimensions of each one—of God's "great" love and "rich" mercy (question 4). This corresponds to the comprehensive power vocabulary in 1:19. Paul's aim seems to be to assure his readers that however dominant and destructive the powers of darkness were in their pre-Christian, pre-conversion experience, the gospel grace and power of God in Christ are superior in every way, so that they have no need to fear or to lack assurance. The immeasurably great power that raised Christ from the dead (1:19-20) is the power that has raised them up with or in Christ.

Question 5 points to three verbs in verses 5-6 that stress the union of the believer "with Christ". God "made us alive", "raised us up" and "seated us with him in the heavenly places", all because we are united to Christ by faith. This is how Paul defines and enlarges on "by grace you have been saved". The three verbs are all in the past tense, so they indicate what has already happened and is already true for every Christian. From God's viewpoint, where Jesus is, there his people are too. Only God can raise the dead, because only he is the author and giver of life. This is precisely what he has done, dealing with our transgressions through the cross and opening up the way to eternal life in God's presence for ever. You will need to underline the difference between the 'now' and the 'not yet' here, which is also implied by Paul's reference to "the coming ages" (v. 7).

Positionally, as far as God is concerned, his people are already 'in Christ', raised to eternal life. That indestructible seed is planted within us here and now, so that Jesus can say, "…whoever hears my word and believes him who sent me has eternal life. He does not come into judgement, but *has* passed from death to life" (John 5:24). And again, "I am the resurrection and the life. Whoever believes in me, though he die, yet shall he live, and everyone who lives and believes in me shall never die" (John 11:25-26). But it will only be in our full enjoyment of the blessings of the eternal kingdom, "in the coming ages", that we shall experience and understand "the immeasurable riches of his grace" and kindness. What we have in a measure here will be ours then in all its fullness, when evil is finally destroyed and we are changed into Christ's likeness completely. Help the group to see that it is all God's grace and kindness, and that it is all available only "in Christ Jesus".

Verses 8-10 return to the emphasis on "faith" as the means by which God's grace is accessed in our lives (question 7). Because faith and faithfulness are interchangeable terms in the original, some commentators suggest that verse 8 refers to the faithfulness of Jesus as the means by which God's saving grace came to operate. This would indicate that our salvation is in no way dependent on us. The "gift of God" is then the faithful obedience of Jesus, humbling himself to do the Father's will, even to death on the cross. But although verse 9 strongly rules out our works as having any part to play in our salvation (and perhaps we should include the saving faith we exercise in Christ as one of these "works"), it seems to be a more inclusive reading to hear Paul teaching that the whole package of salvation, by grace through faith, is God's gracious gift, unearned and totally undeserved. If we take seriously the description of verse 1 that we were dead, we have no problem in realizing that even the faith which unites us to Christ is God's gift, as is every other blessing of the gospel.

Verse 10 then provides a fitting and thrilling conclusion to the study (question 8). We do not work for our salvation; we were "dead", as we have seen. God recreates us, gives us new life, planting the seed of the eternal life in our souls and mortal bodies. God does this work of new creation, and the reality of this miracle of grace is seen in a life of obedience to God, fulfilling the purposes for which he made us, which are the "good works" of these verses. The new creation will produce good works, but it is not produced by them. They are the evidence of justifying faith, not the cause. The rest of the letter will increasingly describe what this new life looks like in practice.

To finish

Because of the comparative familiarity of this favourite passage, there is a danger that the study will only have a 'wash-over' effect for the group. It is deeply humbling when we admit how desperate our state was before Christ found us, and how total is our present (and future) dependence on his grace and mercy. The more we can really appreciate the radical change signified by "But God…" (v. 4), the more our hearts will overflow with thanksgiving and be motivated to do the good works God has prepared for us. So don't be content with merely ticking the doctrinal boxes; ask him for a deep work of his renewing grace that results in trust and obedience.

4. ONE NEW MAN

Ephesians 2:11-22

▶ Remember 60/40/20

 Getting started

It is a contemporary evangelical scandal that there are so many unnecessary divisions between gospel people over everything from music styles in church to personality empire-builders calling for blind followers. This question is designed to get the group thinking about when division is necessary (e.g. Gal 1:6-9) and when not. It sows the seed-thought that to be true gospel Christians we should do everything we can to demonstrate in practice the "one new man" (Eph 2:15), the unity of the one church, which is Christ's body.

Studying the passage

If 2:1-10 focuses on the individual believer and the revolutionary changes in personal life brought about by the gospel, this passage follows the same pattern but in the corporate context of life within the church, God's new society.

It begins with a call to Gentile believers to remember what their condition actually was when God's grace reached out to them. The descriptive terms of verse 12 are very stark—"separated... alienated... strangers... having no hope". We easily become over-familiar with the blessings of the gospel—so it is good to reflect on what these stark descriptions imply and what the realities of life in such a situation really are (question 2).

"But now..." (v. 13) parallels "But God..." (v. 4) and marks the turning point of the paragraph. "Brought near" (v. 13) was a term used to describe Gentiles who became converts to Judaism, but this is so much richer and deeper, not least because of the cost. The person (Christ) and work (his blood shed on the cross) are the only means of personal access to God for previously excluded Gentiles.

We are familiar from elsewhere in Paul's writings with the idea of peace with God through Christ's death on the cross (e.g. Romans 5), but here the emphasis is on peace with one another (questions 3-5). The idea that the cross is the means by which Jews and Gentiles become one new humanity, through faith, is the central concept of verses 14-17. It is an indication of the power of the gospel to demolish human barriers and to create a redeemed community of saved sinners in place of the warring factions of human selfishness.

The "wall of hostility" (v. 14) is probably the Jewish law, which marked them out from the rest of humanity and was often regarded as implying a superiority to the Gentile 'sinners' and 'dogs'. So the law (Torah) produced one of the great divisions of the first-century Mediterranean world. But the law covenant with its sacrificial system is no longer a barrier because Christ has broken it down. Since Christ has perfectly fulfilled the law in his sinless life, and become the once-for-all sacrifice for sin by his atoning death, the law is nullified and the enmity abolished. Both Jews and Gentiles who believe are now on the common ground of the new covenant, by God's grace through the cross. There is no longer any dividing wall between them. Note the full dimensions of this transforming reality. Christ "*is* our peace" (v. 14) because he *made* peace (v. 15) and so he "*preached* peace" (v. 17), through the apostles of the gospel whom he commissioned.

Verse 16 employs a double meaning of the phrase "one body". The physical body of Jesus crucified is the locus of our reconciliation, both to God and to one another. But that makes all who trust in his sacrificial death into one body, one new redeemed humanity, of which Christ is the head (4:15-16). This new unity is experienced and also expressed by our united access to the Father, through the work of the Son and by the enabling of the Holy Spirit.

As the paragraph ends, Paul draws the contrasts of what Gentile believers now are "in him" compared with their previous precarious situation (v. 12). The temple imagery (vv. 21-22) reminds us that in the Old Testament this was the place where God revealed his glory, met with and dwelt among his people—a place from which Gentiles were excluded. That has now been fulfilled in the Lord Jesus Christ, who becomes in himself the meeting place between God and man. Now, united to him by faith, the church of Jews and Gentiles takes on the identity in time and space (and for all eternity) of the dwelling place of God, "a holy temple". Note that this is only "in the Lord" (v. 21) and "by the Spirit" (v. 22). The apostles and prophets (both New Testament) are the foundation gifts that enable the living community to be built on "the cornerstone" (v. 20; see also 3:5 and 4:11). The paragraph has taken us from being "in the flesh"

(v. 11) to being indwelt "by the Spirit" (v. 22).

 ## To finish

To tolerate unnecessary divisions among true gospel believers is a denial of the cross of Christ. It can happen in our churches, where divisions over trivial things spring up. It can happen between churches over secondary matters. We tend to regard these splits and contentions as merely unfortunate, but they actually constitute a scandal, because they run counter to the unity that Jesus established at the cross. God's purposes for unity will certainly be fulfilled in the age to come—however, we must be proactive in seeking to demonstrate that reality here and now, as God's new humanity, in spite of the fallenness of our world and the sinfulness of our nature. The church is the prototype in time of what God will achieve in eternity.

5. MANIFOLD WISDOM

Ephesians 3

▶ Remember 60/40/20

 Getting started

Don't be afraid of getting down to what might seem mundane and unimportant details as you encourage group members to share about their current needs. There are two dangers here: either we think the details of our lives cannot matter to the ruler of the universe, and so we keep our worries and fears from God and try to deal with them without having to 'bother' him; or we become so obsessed with the details of our own lives that we fail to set them in the context of God's universal and eternal purposes, and so we end up trying to run our own show, missing out on so much that could be ours in Christ.

Studying the passage

Verses 2-13 form yet another of Paul's mammoth sentences in the original. They also form a parenthesis that deals with the apostle's gospel ministry to the Gentiles and its place in God's ultimate big picture. The thought begun in verse 1 is not revisited until verse 14, which leads into the second great example of intercessory prayer in the letter.

In verse 1, Paul addresses his readers again as "you Gentiles" (see also 2:11). His apostolic commission to preach the gospel to them (v. 2) is the reason for his imprisonment, but he reminds them that it is entirely a product of God's grace "for you". Indeed, the purpose of the letter is the same as that of Paul's whole ministry—to reveal the "mystery" of the gospel (see 1:9-10, 2:14-16). God's initiation of all this, in grace (v. 2) and by revelation (v. 3), stresses to the Ephesians how important the issues of their own faith and discipleship are in God's eternal purposes (question 1).

The "mystery" now revealed (vv. 3-4) signifies something that was once hidden but has now been revealed—what we might call an 'open secret'. The point is that it never would have been discovered or guessed, had God not chosen to make it known. It is all about Christ (vv. 4, 6)—who he is and what he has done. So a new era has dawned, in which the once-hidden secret about the universal salvation achieved by Christ in the gospel has been revealed to the apostles and New Testament prophets (question 2). Verse 5 refers back to 2:20, where these gifts are described as the foundation of his church. Note that it is the Spirit's work to give insight and to reveal these worldwide dimensions of the good news (see 1:8).

Verse 6 is a climactic revelation (question 3). In Christ, especially through his death and resurrection, Gentile believers are fellow heirs, fellow members and fellow partakers with Jewish believers of God's covenant promises. The fulfilment of all that God promised Abraham, back in Genesis 12:1-3, has now become the new birthright of believing Gentiles.

In verse 7, Paul reflects on how this truth has defined his own life and ministry, with the characteristically Ephesian emphasis on "power". That same dynamic that raised Christ and exalted him (1:20) now empowers his apostle's Gentile mission. Paul received grace (vv. 2, 7), which chose and commissioned him to the work of the gospel (question 4). As a consequence, the Gentiles have received Christ and his "unsearchable riches" (v. 8). The ministry of grace (v. 2) is the ministry of the gospel "mystery" (v. 9), which reveals believing Jews and Gentiles perfectly reconciled to one another because they have been reconciled to God in Christ.

Question 5 focuses on 3:10, which is a key verse to the whole epistle; indeed, some would say it is the message of Ephesians in a nutshell. We might say that God's many-coloured wisdom is made known in the gospel of free grace—and that is certainly so. But Paul takes it a step further and says, "Look what that grace has produced, in the church!" The multiracial, multicultural reality that is the church (with all its imperfections) is the prototype in time of what God will accomplish in eternity. The church is "God's pilot scheme for the reconciled universe of the future" (as FF Bruce once put it).[1] To all the hostile powers in the heavenlies (see 6:12), it is the indisputable declaration that they are totally defeated. They cannot win. Note the emphasis in verse 11 on the "eternal purpose" of the eternal God, and all centred in our Lord Jesus Christ (his full title is used).

Verses 12-13 develop two immediate and practical applications. Access to

God (freedom of entry) with confidence (freedom of speech) is now open to every one of God's people (v. 12), since no hostile powers can thwart the Lord's purposes. This encouragement is then matched by verse 13. Paul's sufferings— the product of God's grace in Gentile gospel ministry—are no cause for discouragement. Rather, they are shown to be for the glory of God's redeemed people and therefore of their glorious redeemer God.

The prayer that follows (vv. 14-21) now picks up these central emphases. Again, verses 14-19 constitute one sentence in the original. The 'oneness' theme is stressed in the address to God as the father of his universal family (vv. 14-15). The very existence of the Gentile church is due to God's glorious riches (v. 16), so Paul asks now that God's riches will continue to be operative in terms of their strength and growth (question 7). He asks that the "power" of the indwelling Spirit will strengthen them as he brings the life of God to transform them from the inside out (v. 16). Following from that (as an outcome of the first request, or possibly as a second request) he asks that they will know that power (v. 18), enabling them to grasp more firmly and enter more deeply into all the dimensions of God's love for them, being filled with God's fullness (question 8; also see 1:23). These might seem to be extravagant requests, but they are more than matched by God's ability ("power") in verse 20. The vocabulary echoes that of verse 18. Note the build-up in verses 20-21: God can do what we *ask*, what we *think*, *all* that we ask or think, *more* than all, indeed *abundantly* more. God's glory is the source (v. 16) and the goal (v. 21) of the indwelling work of God's Spirit, through the sin-bearing work of the cross of Jesus.

God's glory is seen in Christ's love for us, not ours for him, and that is why it "surpasses knowledge" (v. 19) in its experience. This is the road to Christian maturity, to know more of his love and power, which transcend our knowledge and imagination (question 9). But the glory that was first revealed in Christ (John 1:14; 2 Cor 4:6) is now revealed in the church (see Eph 1:6, 12, 14) and will be forever (v. 21). Amen!

To finish

Paul clearly longs for his readers to have such growing and deepening confidence in God's powerful ability to fulfil all his promises and purposes that they would be steadfast in the face of all that the hostile, pagan culture of occult Ephesus might throw at them. It may be good at the end of the study to revisit the anxieties and personal needs expressed in the 'Getting started' section, and to ask how what we have learned in the study about how Christian people are at the very centre of God's plans for time and eternity should now help to change our thoughts and attitudes. Take some of the specific examples that were raised and try to relate the truths of the chapter to them. How has our view of God been expanded (his power and his love) and how does that impact our perspective on our current problems and everyday issues?

1. FF Bruce, *The Epistle to the Ephesians*, Pickering and Inglis, Toronto, 1961, p. 321.

6. ACTIVE UNITY

Ephesians 4:1-16

▶ Remember 60/40/20

 Getting started

It would be easy for this to degenerate into a spell of navel-gazing! On the one hand, if times are currently hard in a local fellowship it could easily precipitate a catalogue of complaints, which become negative whingeing. On the other hand, you will not want to encourage a self-satisfied, mutual admiration society. So the leader will need to balance the contributions, aware of the dangers but also encouraging honesty, and with an overall emphasis on thankfulness.

Studying the passage

While it would be over-simplistic to divide Ephesians into two halves and label chapters 1-3 'doctrine' and chapters 4-6 'practice', it is nevertheless clear that we have now reached the turning point of the epistle. The ground has been laid in the first three chapters, although there is plenty of application built into its structure. Now Paul's attention is much more on the outworking of his teaching in the congregational life of the churches to whom he is writing. This is a strong biblical principle that is clearly exemplified in Ephesians—namely, that commands are only made on the basis of promises; that imperatives require preaching indicatives; or more simply that life-changing practice will only emerge as a result of faithful biblical teaching.

The reference to imprisonment in verse 1 is not just an echo of 3:1 and 13, but also reiterates the urgency of the lifestyle that Paul is about to exhort his readers to embrace. He is a prisoner for the sake of "you Gentiles", but he has only one Lord. Paul is Christ's prisoner, for his sake (3:1, 4:1), and if that is not to be in vain then his readers must be taught, encouraged and exhorted to live a worthy life. These things are not optional extras, but essential Christianity. Moreover, the final teaching section (in the intercessory prayer of 3:14-19) majored on growth in love, experiencing more and more of the unfathomable depths of God's love for us in Christ. But the evidence of the reality of that progress will be seen in a development of love for one another, within the church (question 1).

Verse 1 may therefore be regarded as the topic sentence for the rest of the letter. Verses 2-3 give some very down-to-earth expressions of what "a manner worthy" will look like in practice. The surprising ingredient is that they are all interpersonal relational qualities rather than the outstanding gifts or fervency of service, which we are often tempted to mistake for 'spiritual maturity' (question 2). It is a healthy corrective. A gifted 'worker' who is not humble, gentle, patient and forbearing is not loving and is not therefore walking in a worthy manner. These are the qualities that will actively build up gospel unity.

It is important to notice that in verse 3 there is a unity that already exists between Christians, which is the gift of God in the gospel. Our task is to strive to maintain that given unity. But in verse 13 there is a unity we have to reach, defined as maturity, "the measure of the stature of the fullness of Christ" (see also 1:23). Building on the God-given unity, which connects us through Christ to one another (see also 2:19-22), the section teaches us ways in which we must always be reaching out towards that deeper unity "of the faith and of the knowledge of the Son of God" (v. 13), which is the proof in time of the power of the transforming love of God, in the person of Christ, for eternity.

In verses 4-6, Paul outlines seven evidences of this divinely-given unity, which is created by our common bond of faith-union with the Lord Jesus. The one body is energized by the one Spirit, under one head, the Lord Jesus, to whom we are united by one faith, symbolized by our one baptism, ruled over and permeated by the one God, who is our one Father (question 3). We belong to one another because we belong to him. So the "all", used four times in verse 6, must refer to all believers—Jews and Gentiles.

In the next section (vv. 7-10), by contrast, the emphasis is on diversity (question 4). However, "each one" is included in the distribution of grace, which is the outcome of Christ's triumph (vv. 7-8). The quotation in verse 8 is from Psalm 68:18. It has a number of possible significances, as the more detailed commentaries will point out. In the psalm, the hero warrior ascends to receive gifts, while in Paul's use here he gives gifts as the fruit of his victory. When Jesus ascended he received the gift of God's grace, which he poured out upon his believing people in the coming of the Holy Spirit at Pentecost (see John

1:16-17; Acts 2:32-33). "So that", as Paul had told the Galatians, "in Christ Jesus the blessing of Abraham might come to the Gentiles, so that we might receive the promised Spirit through faith" (Gal 3:14). All this underlines the earlier emphasis on the fruit of Christ's conquest over all the hostile powers and ascension to the place of supreme (cosmic and eternal) authority (v. 10; also see 1:22-23, 3:19). Verse 9 ("descended") refers to his earthly incarnation, rather than to Hades.

Examples of the grace-gifts are then given (v. 11). Apostles and prophets are foundational (see 2:20 and 3:5) and needed before the completion of the canon of the New Testament. But see the emphasis in Hebrews 1:1-4 on the completed word and finished work of Jesus. Evangelists and pastor-teachers continue in every generation. Their purpose is edification of the body (question 5). Biblical ministry is always others-focused and never self-serving. Its aim is to equip others and its effectiveness is seen in developing unity, which is the product of maturity and developing into more and more character-likeness to Christ. The tarnished image of God is being renewed in his people (see 2 Cor 3:18).

The final verses (14-16) alert us to some of the ways in which the enemy forces will seek to disrupt and destroy God's work in and through the church, and how to counteract them. An immature church will be blown about by false teaching and unscrupulous religious operators, so the pastor-teacher's role is vital if God's people are to be "equipped" for service. "Truthing in love" leads to maturity "into Christ", who is the Truth of God incarnate. He is the source of all spiritual growth. His energy holds the body together and energizes its united activity. Note the continuous present tenses in verses 15-16, indicating that this task is never-ending in each generation. Love is the dynamic (v. 16b). Indeed, there cannot be an active, united congregation, in biblical terms, if there is not love between its members.

To finish

In general discussion about the application of this majestic passage, it would be good to admit freely how often the manifestation of Christ's church, in local congregations today, can appear to fall far short of God's ideal. Between both denominations and local congregations there is often rivalry, envy and criticism. We do not often think of this as sin by the members against the body's head. But if we take seriously the thesis of Ephesians—that biblical unity in the gospel is a demonstration of the reality of God's love before a watching (and sceptical) world—we shall not underestimate its importance. Today, divisions occur over relatively minor doctrinal emphases, over dogmatic insistence on aspects of church government or practice, or over some particular Christian experience which is either embraced, or resisted, but in which both sides want to squeeze every other believer into their mould.

All human attempts to solve these differences are bound to fail. The unity for which Christ prayed (see John 17:20-23) and which Paul taught is "the unity of the Spirit" (v. 3) leading to "the unity of the faith" (v. 13). Oneness of faith leads to oneness of life. Unity is only possible in and through the truth of the gospel, which is God's purpose. It is not the fruit of human plans and mechanisms. If we believe this, then we of all people should be passionate about preserving and extending this active gospel unity. What are we doing, actively, to achieve this end? Ask the group to suggest practical ways in which their own unity can be deepened and enriched, and to think how your own fellowship can link up with and encourage other like-minded congregations within your area.

1. 'Pastors' and 'teachers' are linked together in the text; the ESV has 'shepherd where the NIV has 'pastor'.
2. The word often translated "equip" (or "prepare") in verse 12 is used in the Gospels about the disciples mending their nets.

7. RENEWED MINDS

Ephesians 4:17-5:2

▶ Remember 60/40/20

 Getting started

This opening question is designed to alert us to the way that our behaviour is inevitably shaped by our thought life. Paul gives the negative pagan examples in 4:17-19 before expounding the radical transformation that knowing Christ brings in the rest of the passage. In an age that exalts feeling above thought and downplays understanding (wisdom) in favour of experience (sensation), we need to be totally persuaded that "the truth is in Jesus" (4:21), and that this is the only way our minds can be renewed and then each part of our lives be transformed.

Studying the passage

In these verses, Paul's describes what it really means to become a Christian, by giving practical examples of the radically transformed behaviour that flows from the grace of God in the gospel.

He begins with the negative (4:17-19) expressed in very forceful language: "this I say and testify... you must no longer..." (4:17). There is to be no more compromise with the old pre-Christian paganism of Ephesus. Paul again uses the verb "walk" in 4:17, emphasizing the determined movement towards a specific goal. For the Gentiles it is a journey of futility or emptiness.

The process revealed here is very instructive (question 2). Empty minds are due to darkened understanding. That ignorance is, in its turn, generated by their hardened hearts, and in the end culminates in unrestrained sensuality and immorality. Tracing the process backwards, we learn that the godlessness of human society is due to hard hearts resisting all knowledge of God, leading to a darkened world view and a foolish, empty mindset. That is why the Gentile world was as it was, and still is (see also Romans 1:18-32).

The contrast is deliberately stark and arresting (4:20). To become a Christian is to have a changed mind, to 'learn' Christ, and 4:21 explains the process (question 4). Hearing about Jesus is swiftly followed by being taught or instructed in the truth of who Jesus is and what he has done—in other words, the gospel (see 1:13). Note the contrast between the callous resistance of the unbelieving heart (4:19) and the willingness to be taught the truth (4:21). It is the difference between the futile minds of 4:17 and the renewed minds of 4:23, and only God can bring it about. But he does it by the declaration of the truth, which is the only way to learn Christ.

Ephesians 4:22-24 is very important for living the Christian life (question 5). This is how the truth 'works' to move us from empty Gentile living (4:17) to living a life of love (5:2). First, we are taught to put off the old self (4:22) because its desires are corrupt (literally, "rotting"). Human desires come from our sinful hearts and are deceitful, because they never can produce what they seem to offer, since they are opposed to the truth "in Jesus". The old "self", living for my desires as though the world revolved around me, has to be replaced by the new (4:24), which is like God. This is not so much a personality change (we remain ourselves) as a new way of living, where the fallen image of God is being restored in his redeemed people. This is seen in a life and a character that reflect God's righteousness and holiness. You know that the old has gone when the new is being increasingly manifested in everyday life. (See also 2 Corinthians 5:14-21 for parallel ideas.)

But the key verse is 4:23. The mind made new is the secret and dynamic of the new lifestyle. Until our thinking is deeply affected, little else can change. All our efforts at self-reform are doomed to failure. We need renewed thinking in order to know God's will and then to embrace it in a desire to become more like Jesus. Our minds are renewed by growing in the knowledge of Christ, as we are taught the Scriptures. That is how we 'learn Christ', and that is why the evangelists and pastor-teachers are the key gifts in building up Christ's body. It is the mind renewed by God's holy word that motivates us to a renewed life, reflecting God's holy character.

The rest of chapter 4 provides us with five practical examples of how our renewed thinking will motivate us to put off the old and put on the new. Each example follows the same pattern of 4:22-24 (question 6).

Falsehood (lying) must be replaced by truthful speech, and the renewed gospel mindset motivates these actions because we realize that in Christ we belong to one another as "members one of another" (4:25). Transformation is not just getting rid of the old—for nature abhors a vacuum—but also displacing it with the new. I know that I am not a liar because I speak the truth.

Similarly, sinful anger that treasures bitterness and revenge is to be replaced by dealing with issues of contention immediately (before sundown), on the gospel motivation that otherwise we will give territory back to the devil as he divides us from fellow believers by our sinful behaviour. Christ came to make us one (4:26-27).

The thief knows that his life has been transformed when he no longer regards possessions as something to snatch from others, but something to be shared with others in need, as the reward of his honest hard work (4:28). Again the motivation of the renewed gospel-mind is the love and unity that Christ died to bring; not living for self, but sharing with others; not living to gain, but gaining to give.

Unwholesome 'rotting' speech must be replaced by speech that builds up and benefits its hearers (4:29) according to their need. So the effect my words have on others will control my speech, since God has given me his Holy Spirit as the mark of his ownership of my life now and the guarantee of my future redemption (4:30).

That is also why all forms of malicious attitudes, words and actions must be put off. They are the polar opposite of the kind, tenderhearted forgiveness that we have enjoyed from God through the gospel (4:31-32).

If the summary of this new life is essentially being like God (4:24), it is hardly surprising that this unit is rounded off by the exhortation to "walk in love", following the example of the Lord Jesus himself (5:1-2). Because we have been (and are) "beloved children", we are to walk in love, step by step, day by day, as our renewed lifestyle. This means following Jesus in offering our lives to God in sacrificial service, which is fragrant to him and freedom for us. When the church begins to live like this, the world begins to grow hungry for the reality it sees exemplified. When the old self manifests itself instead, the world rightly dismisses the church as a club of pious, religious hypocrites. Renewed minds produce a transformed lifestyle, which is the positive demonstration and proof on earth of God's masterplan for eternity.

 # To finish

It will probably be most helpful to end the study by following Paul's practical examples and perhaps expanding their range. Working through the five examples, the group can be encouraged to express their own difficulties and challenges in these areas of life today. How can the gospel mindset nerve, encourage and motivate us to make the necessary changes of putting off and putting on? Are there other areas, not specifically mentioned here, where either personally or as a group we find ourselves easily compromising the new gospel lifestyle? If these are identified, how can we help one another to apply gospel motivations so that we see these areas as projects of faith, rather than monuments of defeat?

In all of this we need to blend God's limitless resources of grace with our human responsibility to access them. If my responsibility is my response to his ability, then look for all the encouragements in the passage which indicate that God has taken the initiative for change to become possible, through the work of the Father, the Son and the Holy Spirit.

8. GODLY LIVING

Ephesians 5:3-21

▶ Remember 60/40/20

 ## Getting started

This is designed to be a positive beginning to a positive and encouraging passage. Instead of concentrating on areas of failure, as we so often do (sometimes rightly), try to pick up the notes of confidence and thankfulness in the passage and encourage members of the group to celebrate the goodness and faithfulness of the Lord in their recent life experience. It is also helpful to analyse just how God's grace has reached us and to rehearse the means by which his victories have been won. This can be a real encouragement to the downcast.

Set the passage in the wider Ephesian context by pointing out the victory Christ has already won through the cross, triumphing over all the hostile powers, dealing with our sin and apportioning his Spirit to all who repent and believe. We can have confidence that there is no spiritual authority or power which can stand before his sovereign rule, and therefore we can live in a hostile world in faith and not in fear.

Studying the passage

The contrast between the old self and the new, which we explored in chapter 4, now broadens into the contrast between light and darkness and ultimately between the church and the world. There is no room for half-heartedness in such a context, any more than one can have one foot in a boat and the other on dry land. This explains why the categories here are so black and white and the content is expressed so forcefully, although the deceiving world will always strive to blur the distinction.

In verses 3-7 the emphasis is undeniably on sexual sin, but not exclusively so. As so often in the Old Testament, sexual immorality is exposed as a primary example of idolatry and these links are firmly established in verses 3-5. In the paragraph to verse 7, the contrast is between the idolatry of greedy me-centred self-gratification and God-centred thanksgiving. There are implicit Christian arguments against idolatry all through the paragraph (what is "proper among saints", "out of place", "do not become partners" with those who are under God's wrath). It will strengthen our obedience to see the spiritual logic entailed in this. Sex, money and power are still the false gods that ensnare the human race. They are powerful and attractive enough to be able to present a true counterfeit to the good life, and seductive enough to be a real and constant danger to the people of God (question 3). The essence of idolatry is to seize God's good gifts without recognizing the One whose gifts they are and in whose world we live, and so to carve out an independence from God. The root of sin is the refusal to let God be God in my life.

There are plenty of empty words and images that can flatter and deceive (v. 6), which are typical of the futile thinking we saw in 4:17. The strong warning of verse 7 is paralleled in verse 11 ("take no part in..."). This is not an exhortation to try to escape from the world. It is still God's world, and we are to be in it to win it (see Paul's argument in 1 Corinthians 5:9-10). But we are to live distinctively different lives as a result of God's grace. Compromise, as a lifestyle, can only mean wrath and exclusion.

In verses 8-14, Paul returns to his earlier argument about the changes God has already brought about in his readers' lives, expressed now in terms of the strong contrast between light and darkness. Note in verse 8 the close connection between being light and walking in the light (question 4). The fruit is produced by the light within (v. 9), and the darkness is exposed by this light. Godly lives are the way in which sin is shown up for the evil it really is, however much it may seek to bury itself in the darkness (vv. 11-14). And because the source of that light is Christ himself—the light of the world (John 8:12)—he is able to give new life to the spiritually dead, so that the darkness is first exposed and then potentially transformed.

The light of revelation reveals the will of God (v. 10), but also shows the pathway of wisdom that flows from that reality (v. 15). Believers are never careless about their lifestyles, because the issues are eternal and the values reflect the character and purposes of God himself (question 6). Christians seek to do God's will and to use their short time in this present evil age to live for his purposes and priorities (vv. 15-17).

Verse 18 skilfully links an example from the darkness (getting drunk) as an illustration of the opposite way of life, living as light in the fullness of God's Spirit (question 7). The parallel is not that of being out of control, as though to be a Spirit-filled believer is a sort of spiritual inebriation. Rather, it is a contrast between being out of control and being under God's control. This verse, taken out of context, has often been used as a pretext, but the Ephesian letter defines its terms for us. The tense is present continuous—neither once for all, nor a series of climactic emotional experiences. This is the normal Christian life, and all the readers are included. The Spirit is the agency by which we may be continually being filled with all the fullness of God, in Christ. This has already been taught in 1:23, 3:19 and 4:13.

The gift of the Spirit is received by every believer at conversion, as Acts 2:38-39 makes clear. This is the fruit of Christ's victory, his greatest gift to his people, the life of God planted within us (Eph 4:7). Jesus' words in John 7:37-39 relate this to the living water of eternal life, which is the experience of the new birth. Because the Spirit is a divine person of the holy Trinity, it is not possible to receive him by percentages. He is either within us or he is not. So the fullness we receive is not more of the Spirit, but that more areas of our lives are filled and controlled by the life of God within us, changing us increasingly into Christ's likeness from the inside out.

The command "be filled" is then followed by a string of present participles in verses 19-21, which depend upon it (question 8). Here is the continuing evidence of being filled with the life of God—singing, making melody, giving thanks and submitting to one another. It is an unexpected list, but it concentrates on gratitude, joy, humility and grace. We might well have written a list of outstanding gifts, or exciting experiences, or successful ministries, but God's evidence of his presence within us is a joyful, thankful life and a respect for the Lord Jesus that seeks to emulate his love.

 ## To finish

It would be good to summarize the study by drawing attention to the blend of human responsibility—walking in the light, walking in wisdom, discovering God's will and being filled by the Spirit—with God's provision, in terms of his revelation of truth through the Scriptures, and the enabling of the Spirit in the Christian's life. Use the opportunity to observe throughout this section how obedience to God's instruction is motivated by understanding the reasons for it. For example, children of the light are to live according to "all that is good and right and true", not only because this pleases the Lord who has redeemed them, but also because the deeds of darkness are fruitless. They produce nothing but death. Or again, Christians are to walk wisely, step by step, throughout life, buying up every opportunity to understand and carry out God's will, "because the days are evil". Every situation we find ourselves in has the potential to be an occasion when the light of Christ within us may expose the darkness that surrounds us. To know that God's estimation of our world and its cultures is in terms of darkness and death will provide a great motivation for our lives to be full of light (Matt 5:16).

9. FAMILY CIRCLES

Ephesians 5:22-6:9

▶ Remember 60/40/20

 Getting started

There is some dispute as to whether this letter was originally written to Ephesus since the name is missing from the leading manuscripts in 1:1, and in 1:15 Paul says he has heard of their faith, which would seem an odd description of a church he has founded. It is probably that the letter was therefore intended for the churches of Asia Minor, since Paul clearly has particular groups in view ("you Gentiles"). However, the whole area was saturated with the worship of Diana or Artemis, and her cult made her the most worshipped deity throughout the entire Ephesian region. So it is not fanciful to see this section as a corrective to the pagan values of the 'Mother Goddess', whose feminine presence dominated the centre of the cultural, economic and religious life of the province. Here is Paul resisting the pressures to conform to the pagan environment in those areas of personal relationships that are most precious and intimate, and where Christian faith is most starkly at war with the prevailing ethos. The parallels to our situation today are amazingly close.

Studying the passage

In 5:22, almost all English translations introduce the imperative "submit", which is actually absent from the original. This absence ties the example of wives back to the governing participle of verse 5:21, "submitting", which itself depends on the command of 5:18 to be continually filled by, or with, the Spirit. In other words, we cannot expect a fallen world to accept these marriage and family values until and unless the gospel of God's grace is first at work to raise the spiritually dead to life (2:4-7). This is change that comes from within, not by the external imposition of what might otherwise appear to be impersonal principles (question 1).

"To submit" is literally "to arrange under", and 5:21 implies that there is a God-given order to life in his world. God gives wives and husbands complementary but very different roles in marriage and family life, in love and harmony. Only the filling with the Spirit can produce this sort of response. Without God's transforming grace, wives will not want to submit and husbands will either not want to lead, or else try to exercise a tyrannical authority. It is important for the group to see that the issue is not one of equality, as it can often be misrepresented. Equality is established in Genesis 1:27-28. Rather, the issue is a matter of different responsibilities and roles (as within the equality of the Trinity—see 1 Corinthians 11:3). A Christian husband is responsible before God for the "one flesh" unit that is his marriage, which he must lead in a Christlike way, as we will see below. Similarly, a Christian wife will show her submission to Christ in her loving, godly submission to her husband. Note too that this is not conditional ("I will if he/she does"). It is an obligation of our discipleship.

The responsibilities of the husband expounded in 5:25-30 are much more demanding, since the love of Christ for his people in self-sacrifice is the pattern for the husband's relationship with his wife (question 3). The emphasis is all on the wife's benefit (5:26-27), which is seen as parallel to the benefits we receive from the Lord Jesus. The essence of love is self-giving for the benefit of the loved one, which is the very heart of the Trinity. But Paul then reminds his readers of the teaching in Genesis 2:24 about the "one flesh" unit, which is God's design and purpose in marriage, so that love for one's wife is love for one's own body, just as Christ's love for the church nourishes and cherishes his body (5:28-31).

In drawing this parallel, we must also be clear that Paul is not saying that a husband must be Christ to his wife. That would be as unhelpful as it is impossible. Ephesians 5:26-27 describes what only the Lord Jesus can do for his people. "The washing of water with the word" must refer to the word of the gospel that provides cleansing (as water does for the body) through the death of Christ for our sins. Similarly, he is the only one who can present his sons and daughters perfect on the last day (5:27). But this analogy provides us with the highest possible aims for our marriages, as Christian wives submit to their husbands, and as Christian husbands sacrificially lay down their own lives for their wives. Echoes of earlier teaching in the letter occur in Paul's use of the term "mystery" (5:32), and in the emphasis on unity and love, which has been the major theme since 4:1. We can only know God's blueprint for marriage because he has chosen to reveal it to us, in all its profundity, and we can only put it into practice by being filled with his Spirit (5:18).

Because Christ is Lord of all (1:22-23), his people must recognize the authority structures he has instituted for the household or family, which marriage creates, and live within them (question 6). The context of 6:1-3 clearly refers to children who are still being brought up in the family home (6:4). To honour one's parents, expressed by obedience (6:1), not only fulfils the commandment in the letter (Exod 20:12) but also in the spirit, because it is the sign of love and reverence for our heavenly Father. Note the motivation: "this is right" (6:1) because it is God's will (see 5:10, 17). Also, as always with our gracious Father, the commandment is accompanied by a promise (6:2-3). Both are characteristic of God, who is both light and love.

Ephesians 6:4 is worth thinking about in more detail (question 7). Fathers are the focus since they are responsible before God for the headship of the family unit, but there are lessons for mothers here too. Children can be exasperated either by absence, lack of interest in them or lack of discipline on the one hand, or by domination, unrealistic demands and excessive controls on the other. Scripture is the corrective—both for the children and the parents.

In dealing with slaves and masters (6:5-9) we have to recognize some discontinuity between the first-century employment system and our labour laws today, however much employees may consider themselves to be slaves! The household context is still the focus in these verses, whereas today most of us leave home to go to work, and the workplace often has only a minimal connection with our family circles. However, there are some key principles here to direct our lives in the workplace so that we live out the gospel authentically and attractively. Again, it is not about equality or inequality. Slaves are addressed as equals with their masters before God (6:9). But out of reverence for Christ they will fulfil their role in obeying their earthly masters, whether Christian or not (see also 1 Peter 2:18-20). In 6:6, eye-service and heart-service are contrasting motivations, revealing comparative degrees of sincerity in their work and lives. Note the emphasis on serving the Lord in 6:5, 6 and 7, with the incentive of his reward (6:8). Similarly, the instruction to masters in 6:9 focuses on the context of heaven and eternity.

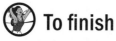 # To finish

As our culture increasingly turns its back on the remnants of its once-Christian heritage, this will inevitably lead to more marriage and family disintegration, with increasingly fractured relationships and broken trust in the world of work. It would be good to talk through and pray about the great gospel opportunities this provides. Loving marriages and families, coupled with dependable and conscientious work practices, will have an increasing magnetism for those whose lives are wounded and hearts sickened by the relationship chaos of the modern world. Christian reality in these areas may well be the most profound and winsome apologetic for the gospel that many of our fellow-citizens will ever encounter. This is one way in which the church reveals "the manifold wisdom of God", in the gospel's transforming power, to all the hostile forces of evil (see again 3:10). But it has to be working! So we need to help one another and pray together that this passage will move from being a magnificent ideal to being the daily fabric of life in our family circles. There is no lack of resources with God (5:18).

10. SPIRITUAL WARFARE

Ephesians 6:10-24

▶ Remember 60/40/20

 Getting started

Many of us forget the context of the spiritual warfare in which we live our lives. The opening question is designed to orientate our thinking to this perspective and help us to be honest about why we sometimes prefer to ignore it. In the Ephesian context of powerful, occult paganism with its fear-ridden culture of spells and curses, magic and demonic powers (remember Acts 19), spiritual warfare was an all-too-obvious and inescapable dimension of daily experience. Paul's readers need to know, understand and believe in the total supremacy of the crucified and risen Lord so that they will stand firmly on what he has accomplished for them, as they fight against the world, the flesh and the devil. Only then will their love be "incorruptible" (v. 24). And it is exactly the same for us today.

Studying the passage

As indicated above, this closing exhortation reintroduces the cosmic perspective, setting the instructions of 4:1-6:9 in that larger context once again. It is the climax of the whole letter and provides convincing and powerful motivation to carry out the commands given and elaborated in this section.

"Be strong" (v. 10) is literally a passive—'be strengthened'. The power that raised Christ from the dead is available to be appropriated by the weakest believer in the struggle against sin and evil. The words of 1:20-21 provide a helpful reminder of the immensity and sufficiency of this divine resource. However, that mighty power becomes ours only as we "put on the whole armour of God" (v. 11). Note that the command is repeated in verse 13. We can only stand because Christ has triumphed. Indeed, the warfare involves such awesomely powerful enemies (v. 12) that it becomes obvious that reliance on merely human resources will prove to be utterly inadequate. This explains why we are so often defeated. We have not accessed God's omnipotence, and so we fail to stand (question 2).

The war is described in verse 12 in terms of hand-to-hand combat; it's a "wrestle". We each have a battle to fight, often on several different fronts, where the enemy is trying to take back the ground that Christ has won for us. Each Christian 'soldier' bears a personal responsibility, but we fight together as God's united people (Christ's body) through Christ's saving work. As the letter has constantly taught, the unity and love of the church is the present declaration and demonstration of Christ's eternal victory (question 3).

Not surprisingly, the "whole armour of God" is described in verses 14-17 in terms of the gospel that introduced the letter back in 1:3-14. Each piece is related to Christ's work on behalf of his people, and each piece takes us back to previous references and earlier teaching in the epistle:

- The belt of truth (v. 14) binds all the soldiers' clothing and equipment together. In 1:13, "the word of truth" is defined as "the gospel of your salvation". This is what makes us Christian soldiers and members of Christ's body. Every spiritual blessing is in Christ alone (1:3) and in his saving work. This truth made personal, by faith, is the foundation of everything else. Without it, we are still dead in trespasses and sins (2:1), "separated from Christ", and without hope and "without God in the world" (2:12). Gospel truth needs to be "put on" every day.

- Righteousness (the breastplate; v. 14) is the mark of the new self, which is being renewed in the image of its creator (4:22-24). This is the new life implanted within us as the light of Christ raises us from the death of sin (5:14). Children of light display the characteristics of the one who has given them birth (5:9). The righteousness this produces was described and explained in 4:25-5:2, and we need to commit ourselves to its development daily as we put off the old and put on the new.

- Preparedness to go on believing and proclaiming this gospel gives God's people a firm footing in the fight, and leads to peace with God and with one another. This theme was the focus of 2:14-18, when Christ, who "is our peace", made peace (2:14-15) by creating one new humanity of believers whether Jews or Gentiles, and then "preached peace" (2:17) for all who will avail themselves of the access to the Father in the Spirit (2:18). This unity of the Spirit (4:3) is secured through the bond of peace, which is again totally dependent on Jesus and his saving work.

- Faith is our defence against the enemy's burning arrows—our shield (v. 16). Again, this has been a major theme through the letter. See 1:13-14, where believing is the key to everything; 1:15 and 19, where faith is the access to God's salvation and power; 2:8, where faith is the mechanism of salvation; 3:12, where it is the ground of our approach to God; and 3:17, where faith is the means by which God's indwelling life is experienced.

- Strength in the battle comes from daily appropriation of God's promises and enjoyment of God's gospel gifts. The "helmet of salvation" (v. 17) protects our minds and the control centre of the personality by reminding us of what we already have in Christ. This has been the continuing thread of the letter from 1:3 onwards. Paul's stress is always on God's initiative (2:5, 8), and the heart of the relationship we have with Christ is that he is our saviour (5:23).

- All these are defensive weapons, but the sword is for attack (v. 17), and this is the function of God's word, inspired by the Holy Spirit. It is the word of God in the hands of the Spirit of God that accomplishes the work of God in his world. As we believe it and proclaim it, the enemy is repulsed.

Prayer (v. 18) is not really a weapon at all but a lifestyle, as the comprehensiveness of the verse indicates (question 6). "Keep alert" is a continuous requirement, which calls for hard work and perseverance ("praying at all times"). From our perspective in the battle, prayer is the channel by which divine enabling comes to us to keep us faithful and true (vv. 19-20).

The rest of the letter has a number of endearing personal references, reminding us that although this may have been a circular letter, Paul was not writing to a totally unknown readership. He asks for prayer for himself, for boldness to go on proclaiming this gospel that he has expounded and which is the cause of his present imprisonment (question 7). There is no sense in which the great apostle sees himself as superior to his readers. He too experiences fear and needs, wisdom and boldness, as we all do. Personal news from Tychicus will encourage them (vv. 21-22), and Paul's parting prayer-wish for them is peace, love with faith (see 1:15) and grace, which are all major gospel themes and major emphases throughout the letter (vv. 23-24).

Love for the Lord Jesus Christ that lasts forever is the surest sign of God's grace received and experienced through the gospel (v. 24). The love Paul is talking about is literally "love with immortality" and so is translated "incorruptible" (ESV) or "undying" (NIV). Note how this final section links back to chapter 1. What God has been praised and petitioned for in chapter 1 is the means by which his people are to be preserved and come through victoriously in this sixth chapter of spiritual warfare. We need to grasp, with the same confidence, the undying truth that the armour of God and the strength of his might are our own more than adequate resources.

To finish

There is great value in seeing the big picture, or hearing the melodic line, of every Bible book. Try to make time to review these ideas in Ephesians as a whole. If you had to choose a key verse to sum up the message, what would it be? 1:10, 1:22-23, 2:6-7, 3:10? All good choices! If you had to sum up its message in a single sentence, what would you want to see included? A favourite summary of the book is to say, "It's all about the church", but we have seen so much more than that. It's about what the church is, and why it is, and how it is central to God's eternal purposes. It's about the gospel's transforming, life-giving power and how the church is the outcrop in time of God's vast, cosmic and eternal plan. And so it's all about Christ, and expanding our vision of him—who he is, what he has accomplished and what he is doing at work in his world today, though his people, empowered by his Spirit. It's about a love that is inexhaustible and unending, lavished upon undeserving rebels, but which produces a transformed community, themselves loving one another and their Lord, Jesus Christ, "with love incorruptible".

matthiasmedia

Matthias Media is an evangelical publishing ministry that seeks to persuade all Christians of the truth of God's purposes in Jesus Christ as revealed in the Bible, and equip them with high-quality resources, so that by the work of the Holy Spirit they will:

- abandon their lives to the honour and service of Christ in daily holiness and decision-making
- pray constantly in Christ's name for the fruitfulness and growth of his gospel
- speak the Bible's life-changing word whenever and however they can—in the home, in the world and in the fellowship of his people.

It was in 1988 that we first started pursuing this mission, and in God's kindness we now have more than 300 different ministry resources being used all over the world. These resources range from Bible studies and books through to training courses and audio sermons.

To find out more about our large range of very useful resources, and to access samples and free downloads, visit our website:

www.matthiasmedia.com

How to buy our resources

1. Direct from us over the internet:
   – in the US: www.matthiasmedia.com
   – in Australia and the rest of the world:
     www.matthiasmedia.com.au

2. Direct from us by phone:
   – in the US: 1 866 407 4530
   – in Australia: 1800 814 360
     (Sydney: 9663 1478)
   – international: +61-2-9663-1478

> Register at our website for our **free** regular email update to receive information about the latest new resources **exclusive special offers,** and free articles to help you grow in your Christian life and ministry.

3. Through a range of outlets in various parts of the world. Visit **www.matthiasmedia.com/contact** for details about recommended retailers in your part of the world, including www.thegoodbook.co.uk in the United Kingdom.

4. Trade enquiries can be addressed to:
   – in the US and Canada: sales@matthiasmedia.com
   – in Australia and the rest of the world: sales@matthiasmedia.com.au

Interactive Bible Studies

Interactive Bible Studies are a bit like a guided tour of a famous city. They take you through a particular part of the Bible, helping you to know where to start, pointing out things along the way, suggesting avenues for further exploration, and making sure that you know how to get home. Like any good tour, the real purpose is to allow you to go exploring for yourself—to dive in, have a good look around, and discover for yourself the riches that God's word has in store.

In other words, these studies aim to provide stimulation and input and point you in the right direction, while leaving you to do plenty of the exploration and discovery yourself.

We pray that these studies will stimulate lots of 'interaction'—interaction with the Bible, with the things we've written, with your own current thoughts and attitudes, with other people as you discuss them, and with God as you talk to him about it all.

FOR MORE INFORMATION OR TO ORDER CONTACT:

Matthias Media
Telephone: +61-2-9663-1478
Facsimile: +61-2-9663-3265
Email: sales@matthiasmedia.com.au
www.matthiasmedia.com.au

Matthias Media (USA)
Telephone: 1-866-407-4530
Facsimile: 330-953-1712
Email: sales@matthiasmedia.com
www.matthiasmedia.com

Pathway Bible Guides

Pathway Bible Guides are simple, straightforward, easy-to-read Bible studies, ideal for groups who are new to studying the Bible, or groups with limited time for study. We've designed the studies to be short and easy to use, with an uncomplicated vocabulary. At the same time, we've tried to do justice to the passages being studied, and to model good Bible-reading principles. Pathway Bible Guides are simple without being simplistic; no-nonsense without being no-content.

Looking for something more?

If you're looking for more input for your Christian life and service, take a look at *The Briefing*.

more diversity

With a variety of columns and sections, and local and overseas perspectives, *The Briefing* offers plenty to readers in various stages and walks of life.

more content

Since *The Briefing* is available not just in print but also online, we can provide lots of content, including audio/video and new hosted blogs by gifted Christian thinkers and writers. Choose the content that is most relevant and useful to you.

more convenient

You can receive *The Briefing* in the way that best suits your reading habits—on the web, as an RSS feed, by pdf, as an email update, on your phone or smart device, and of course in print.

more social

Being online, *The Briefing* is share-able and discuss-able. So it's simple to connect your friends into *The Briefing* content via your favourite social networks.

more free

The remarkable thing about *The Briefing* is that it is *all* available free. Of course, if you want to have the beautiful paper edition mailed out to you then there is a small charge.

more information?

All the information you're likely to need, including subscription options, can be found at: **www.matthiasmedia.com/briefing**